CHRISTOPHER COLUMBUS

Sailing to America

Jane Bingham

FACT CAT

Get your paws on this fantastic new mega-series from Wayland!

Join our Fact Cat on a journey of fun learning about every subject under the sun!

Published in paperback in 2017 by Wayland
© Hodder and Stoughton 2017

Wayland
An imprint of
Hachette Children's Group
Part of Hodder & Stoughton
Carmelite House
50 Victoria Embankment
London EC4Y 0DZ

Produced for Wayland by
White-Thomson Publishing Ltd
www.wtpub.co.uk
+44 (0) 843 208 7460

Editor: Jane Bingham
Design: Rocket Design (East Anglia) Ltd
Fact Cat illustrations: Shutterstock/Julien Troneur
Other illustrations: Stefan Chabluk
Consultant: Kate Ruttle

A catalogue for this title is available from the British Library

ISBN: 978 0 7502 9033 3
ebook ISBN: 978 0 7502 9032 6

Dewey Number: 970'.015'092-dc23

10 9 8 7 6 5 4 3 2 1

Wayland is a division of Hachette Children's Group,
an Hachette UK company.
www.hachette.co.uk

Printed and bound in China

FSC MIX Paper from responsible sources FSC® C104740

Picture and illustration credits:
Stefan Chabluk 4, 9, 13, 17, 18, 20; Library of Congress 16,19; Wikimedia 5,6,7,10,12; Valentin Volkov/Shutterstock 8; Henner Damke/Shutterstock 1, 11; Jiri Miklo/Shutterstock 14 (1); Egor Rodynchenko Shutterstock 14 (2); diamant24/Shutterstock 14 (3); Jiang Hongyan/Shutterstock 14 (4); Jiang Hongyan/Shutterstock 14 (5); Radekdrewek/Dreamstime 15; spirit of america/Shutterstock 21.

Every effort has been made to clear copyright.
Should there be any inadvertent omission,
please apply to the publisher for rectification.

The author, Jane Bingham, is a writer and editor specialising in children's educational publishing.

The consultant, Kate Ruttle, is a literacy expert and SENCO, and teaches in Suffolk.

FACT CAT FACT

There is a question for you to answer on each spread in this book. You can check your answers on page 24.

CONTENTS

WHO WAS COLUMBUS?

Christopher Columbus was a great explorer. In 1492 he sailed west from Europe. Seventy days later, he reached the **continent** of North America!

This map shows Columbus's **voyage** in 1492. He explored a group of islands off the coast of North America.

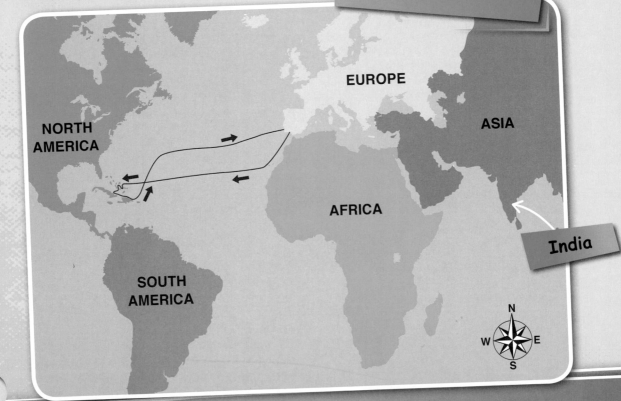

EUROPE

ASIA

NORTH AMERICA

AFRICA

India

SOUTH AMERICA

N
W · E
S

Columbus never knew he had reached North America. Instead, he believed he had found a new **route** to **Asia**.

Columbus sailed to America four times! He died soon after his last voyage. Can you find out how old he was when he died?

FACT CAT FACT

Columbus thought he had reached some islands near India. So he called them the Indies. Later, people called them the West Indies.

YOUNG COLUMBUS

Columbus was born in Genoa, in northern Italy. As a young man, he worked as a sailor. But when he was 25 he nearly drowned. His ship was attacked by an enemy **warship**.

Columbus decided to stop being a sailor for a while. He lived in Portugal and worked as a map-maker.

In Columbus's time, world maps were not very **accurate**. Large parts of Africa hadn't been explored and America was completely unknown.

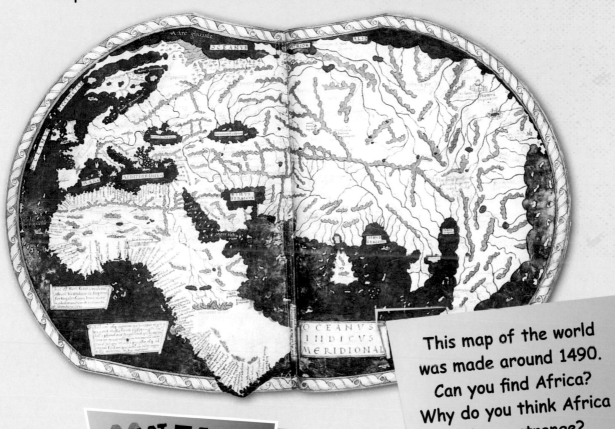

This map of the world was made around 1490. Can you find Africa? Why do you think Africa looks so strange?

FACT CAT FACT

In the 1400s, many people believed the Earth was flat. They thought ships could fall off the edge of the Earth!

THE VOYAGE BEGINS

Columbus asked the King of Portugal to pay for his voyage, but the king refused. So Columbus turned to the rulers of Spain for help.

Spain was ruled by King Ferdinand and Queen Isabella. They supported Columbus because they wanted to find an easier way for traders to reach Asia.

On 3 August 1492 three ships left Spain. They were the *Santa Maria*, the *Nina* and the *Pinta*. After just three days at sea, the *Pinta* was damaged.

This is a copy of the *Santa Maria*, Columbus's biggest ship. Can you find out how long it was?

FACT CAT FACT

Columbus's ships carried lots of food for the sailors. There were even some live pigs and chickens!

EXPLORING THE ISLANDS

Columbus found many colourful plants on the islands. He saw amazing animals, birds and insects.

The **islanders** ate fruits and vegetables that the sailors had never seen before. Can you name the foods shown here?

1

2

3

4

5

The Taíno people lived on Hispaniola. Some of their **descendants** still live in the West Indies.

This man is a **member** of the Taíno people.

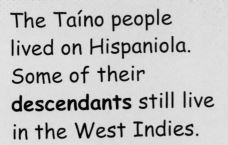

FACT CAT **FACT**

Some Taíno words have become part of the English language. **Barbecue**, **hammock**, **hurricane** and **canoe** all come from the Taino language.

MORE AdVENTURES

On Christmas Eve 1492, the *Santa Maria* was **wrecked**. Columbus decided it was time to head for home. He left 39 men on Hispaniola, but he promised to return.

Columbus was welcomed in Spain as a hero. He brought gifts of gold, plants and parrots. He also brought some islanders back with him. How many islanders travelled to Spain?

Ferdinand and Isabella wanted more treasure. So they paid for Columbus to sail west again. In 1493, he set out on his second voyage.

Columbus reached the small island of Dominica. Then he continued to Puerto Rico, Hispaniola, Cuba and Jamaica.

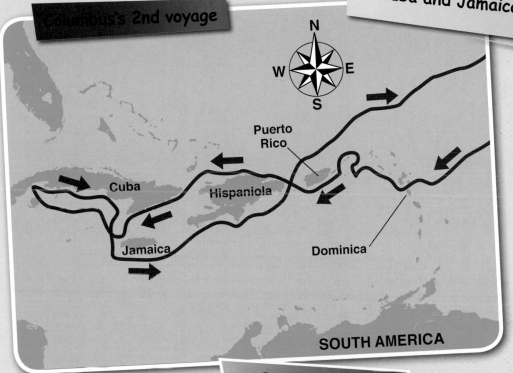

Columbus's 2nd voyage

N
W   E
S

Puerto Rico

Cuba

Hispaniola

Jamaica

Dominica

SOUTH AMERICA

FACT CAT FACT

Columbus took 17 ships on his second voyage. The ships carried more than a thousand Spanish people to **settle** on the islands.

COLUMBUS IN TROUBLE

In 1498, Columbus left Spain with six ships. Three ships headed straight to Hispaniola. Columbus sailed further south with the other ships.

On Columbus's third voyage, the wind died down completely. His ships **drifted** for eight days before they could sail again.

Columbus's 3rd voyage

Columbus reached the island of Trinidad. Then he sailed north to Hispaniola.

Hispaniola

Trinidad

SOUTH AMERICA

When Columbus reached Hispaniola, the Spanish **settlers** were fighting amongst each other. Many people blamed Columbus for the fighting.

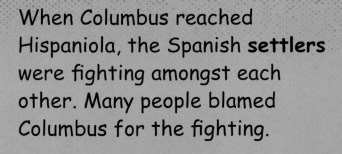

Columbus was sent home in chains, but he was later **forgiven**. In which year was he sent back to Spain?

COLUMBUS'S LAST VOYAGE

On his fourth voyage, Columbus sailed along the coast of America. But his ships were badly damaged in storms. He landed on Jamaica just as his last ship fell apart.

A sailor set out from Jamaica in a canoe. He headed for Hispaniola to find help. One year later, Columbus was rescued and he returned to Spain.

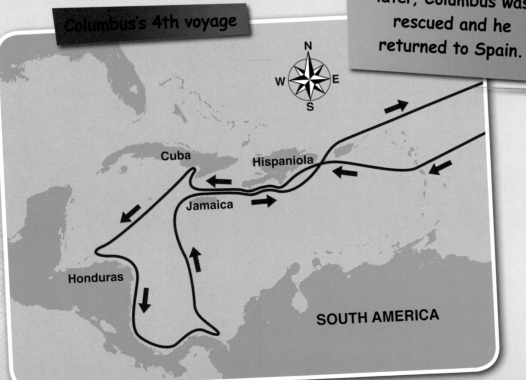

Columbus's 4th voyage

N
W E
S

Cuba

Hispaniola

Jamaica

Honduras

SOUTH AMERICA

When Columbus reached home he was tired and ill. He died two years later. Even at the end of his life, he still thought he had reached Asia. He never guessed he had found a new continent.

Every October in the USA, people celebrate Columbus Day. They remember the day when Columbus reached the continent of North America. There are two flags in this photo. Which countries do they **represent?**

QUIZ

Try to answer the questions below. Look back through the book to help you. Check your answers on page 24.

1 How many times did Columbus sail to America?

a) four times

b) twice

c) six times

2 Ferdinand and Isabella paid for Columbus's voyages. Which country did they rule?

a) Italy

b) Portugal

c) Spain

3 Columbus reached Asia. True or not true?

a) true

b) not true

4 On his last voyage Columbus had to wait on an island for a year. Which island was it?

a) Dominica

b) Hispaniola

c) Jamaica

5 Columbus died in the West Indies. True or not true?

a) not true

b) true

GLOSSARY

accurate exactly right

anchor a heavy metal hook that is lowered from a ship or boat to stop it floating away

Asia the continent that includes India, China and Japan

barbecue a special fire for cooking meat

bay a long beach that curves inwards

canoe a long, narrow boat that is moved through the water by using a wooden paddle

continent one of the seven large masses of land on the Earth. Europe, Asia and North America are all continents

descendants people who belong to a family or tribe with a long history

distance the amount of space between two places

drift move without a clear direction

forgiven no longer blamed or in trouble

hammock a bed made from rope or cloth and hung from its two ends

hurricane a very strong storm

islanders people who live on an island

journal a diary in which people write what they have done and seen each day

look-out boy a boy on a ship whose job is to look for any sign of land

member someone who belongs to a group or an organization

merchant someone who exchanges goods with traders from other countries

represent stand for something

route a way of getting from one place to another

settle make a home in a new country

settlers people who make their home in a new country

shore the edge of the land, where it meets the sea, a river or a lake

spices parts of plants that are used to add flavour to food

voyage a journey by sea

warship a ship that is used in battles

wreck break into pieces

INDEX

ANSWERS

Pages 5–21

page 5: Columbus died aged 54.

page 7: Africa looks strange because the map was made before explorers from Europe had sailed round it.

page 9: Vasco da Gama sailed around Africa to India in 1498.

page 11: The Santa Maria was about 15 to 18 metres (50 to 60 feet) long.

page 13: Hispaniola is made up of Haiti and the Dominican Republic.

page 14: The foods are: (1) pineapple; (2) chillies; (3) pepper; (4) potato; (5) sweet potato.

page 16: Six islanders travelled to Spain.

page 19: Columbus was sent back to Spain in chains in 1500.

page 21: The flags represent Italy (where Columbus was born) and the USA.

Quiz answers

1   a) Columbus sailed to America four times.

2   c) Ferdinand and Isabella ruled Spain.

3   b) not true

4   c) Jamaica

5   a) not true